Simply Stabbed by a Brush Stroke

By Matt Burrus

To: Amy Ouimet
Pressed between these pages
there is angst, boredom, fear and frustration,
But there is also joy.
Thank you for being interested in reading
this, I hope there is something in here
for everyone.

-Matt

A Collection of 119 Poems written by Matt Burrus from 2013 to 2016

Cover Art by Katie Romansky, 2016.
Katie is a geologist/ climber/ artist from Calgary AB. She is an amazing, meticulous artist and you would be clever to explore and support her work at (@katiero_) on instagram.

(The old man sits in the grass
ahead of his time)

It is said that who you currently are, is a result of all of your past selves/ages added together and built one upon the other.

This book is dedicated to my past selves; all of my selves in past years that have existed scared and alone and rejected. There is so much growth that can happen if you allow yourself to experience it.

This book is a linear progression of a selection of some of the poetry that I have written, starting in 2013 while I was still attending college. It follows me through two cities, two breakups, thousands of liters of coffee and many late night walks. I decided it was completed in 2016 when I realized that I needed to live through painful experiences, however uncomfortable, to grow.

I am excited for you to join me in this messy book.

-Matt

Grabbing the sky in one hand
the earth in another

I pull the atmosphere towards me

Crushing myself
under healthy oxygen

all the way there
my lungs filled with out-dated air
where a second ago, it was all that I needed

but the need for something new to replace the old
grows in my lungs as in the world
I breathe out, unable to hold onto the past

a release of the past repeated over and over
each breath a vital forgotten cog
that turns closer to its final rotation

Deep Breathing is the key

Every Iota of strength required
Even the smallest thought a negative neuron
Pulse Cannon firing in the wrong direction

..........Thinking slows you down

Straining my voice to be heard,
I yell across a sea of sound.

This microscopic parasite
is nothing compared to the nebula surrounding it.

Willow trees cry at the stars

White wine spills on red carp
Beachcombers find turtles addresses carved into a driftwood

A fruit fly's imagination
Coyotes discuss history with the magic Lemons
The love of one rock to another makes the mountains hum

The love of the simple is the greatest joy

I feel the ground
Don't mind me…

The world looks better vertically
Don't mind me..

Inwardly I'm screaming
Don't mind me.

Hardly feel my head
Don't mind.

Found my voice at last
Don't.

Slender tree fingers

Wave to me in the white morning.

A familiar old man greets me

At the door.

We share coffee on the front steps

My breath a large cloud

Sitting together in the snow

Take steel around your ears
Write with air on the sides of train cars
While I stare against the sky
Paint without ever looking
Never look at what you do
But I can't stop watching

Meet me under the snow steeped trees
At night when the light is as soft as down

Light is a dream we were never meant to wake from
Here in the snow the dream goes on forever

Meet me among the statues of ice and light

Floodlights on, these nights
Hanging on to the cold dream of moonlit peaks
Watch your batteries and gas tanks
Deplete into the darkness
Fade Fade Fade off and away….
Only when it's dark enough
Will clouds give way to stars

Let yourself grow, sit and drink time like a rare tea

For we are simple, our lives like those of mayflies
Quick and easily forgotten

A shrill song in the wind
Blown away

You accidentally catch a glimpse of yourself in a mirror
But the face you see is dated 70 years in the future

Crows feet, bags, permanent dimple creases, grey scraggly hair...
All reflect an existence that you have yet to experience.

But the existence of loss is the clearest emotion that your face conveys.
People that you love are gone in the future, leaving scars that show only in your eyes

The Fear of Lost Paint

Don't let it hurt you
the fear of the unknown
The missed 'possibilities'
In your future

The spectrum of colour
Is laid out before you
Can you predict
Every painting yet to be made?

Life's possibilities are the spectrum
Every shade is not needed
To make a master painting

Passing through towards another
Lay your head down
Transfer

Magnify into another verse
Live again while you sleep
Dream

It's so easy to ignore the laws of physics
By walking into other lives

When the mind flickers active
Your body stops
Transfer

Wake and feel
The past is past
Dream

I watched a seal walk by me, late to a business meeting
Flowers asked me what day it was
A little drunk sparrow told me that life wasn't worth living anymore
'This is incredible!' said a grizzly bear after taking a new car for a spin.
Humans are the only living things that do this
And we think we are 'normal'

A picture of my room from grade 1 hangs
on a hook nailed to my bedroom door

A before and after view
every time I enter, reminds me that

The future always changes
but the past stays the same.

A balding middle-aged man sitting next to me is talking about watching Cosmos.
I can see his Adam's apple bob up and down as he talks.
I am sitting at a table draped in eraser shavings, like a light dusting of snow.
There is no more snow outside anymore, just gravel left over when the ice melted away.
Gravel and dust coats everything in this place, well in addition to the eraser shavings.
I should go watch Cosmos. [1]

---

[1] I wrote this while studying for my 2014 Government Exams in Selkirk College, basically a plan to procrastinate.

"All in all we're just another brick in the wall…"

Except for you. Yes you.

You are that brick from National Treasure with the really cool 3D glasses. [2]

---

[2] This was the first time I saw any external interest in my writing, and it was because of something I thought up in the shower.

I met a man yesterday in a climbing gym who was quietly awesome.

A Forestry specialist like my dad used to be.

Management was angry with him because the expiry date was not included on his punch pass.

"People come in here without dates on passes that are years old!" the lady said, clearly angry that people would try to scam her.

The man said nothing until the lady started to walk away.

"Well" he said, "That means this place keeps old friends coming back for years."

I'm on fire for the day
All of my useless defences burned away
Small comforts, nothing of value in the end
Stark and cold
Naked with my thoughts
Peering into the night my mind transformed into.

life is my currency.
not a game.

I will not play it to gain wealth.
I will spend it to promote happiness
in myself and others.

See

Watch the sun set into my hand

I'll wash it down with a sea of sand

And save it for another day

Save it for another rainy

lifetime away

Shiver in the sun

Watch the grasses burn
I lost my name in a freak accident.
Only the sound of a million birds calling for a mate

Will make me remember again.
Hopefully soon I can move on
It feels like I've been sitting here forever.

Loving the space I occupy
Just alright to stay where I am

An unending drive is needed, people say
But this leaves me forever wanting more, never satisfied.
I can't always be looking onwards
It's a waste of my present time.

I'm going to take a nap in the sun
It's worth it.

one one one one

two never more

one one one

ever glide onward

one one

at most see the worst in others

one

living in the rafters.

Enter into timelines not your own

See your mother with your math teacher
Your dad with the fast gas clerk.

Both happy
Both where they want to be

You don't exist in ninety precent of alternate timelines
Nevertheless everything functions fine.

The universe doesn't need you, the opposite is true
Live without fear, it will soon be over.

But fear not going the distance with this small plot of
time you temporarily have

Feeling disconnected some circuit popped or wire broken
Emotional energy flowed through me until I fizzled out.
Not a single emotional feeling.
I evaporate onto the ceiling…
No one can make me feel
A needed break from all this traffic in my heart and head.

They will come back
She said

The mirrors floating beside your head.
In other people's eyes

See the end of a thousand days of winter
In your heart, the ache to feel anything at all…

Drowns out the sounds of distraction.

A dark day dawns down Death's driveway.
A grim grey gravelled graveyard without grass sits atop it.
Death slides sadly into studded stiletto heels and sighs.

Whitewashed walkways watch the whites of his eyes
walk around the graveyard and then back to the heels.

Death rises and replies to a mirror on the biggest
tombstone to his right.

"I'm not going to be alright"

Warm air swirls around my feet
Like ocean swells in summer storms

Thunder from above
Lifts me from the hill

Rain mixed at forty thousand feet
Washes my hair

The lightning charge tickles my fingers
Then they explode

Shattered body
With lips that tasted the sun

Lay down
In the melted sand

Torn, broken, alive.

Ask my meaningless opinion
Symmetry in feelings
Positives balanced with negatives

Take not from me my fears
For they remind me I am mortal.

Take not from me my insecurities
For they teach me to understand others.

Take not from me my cynicism
For it provides a clear window into life.

Take from me my joy
I shall find it again

Take from me my accomplishments
They do not define me

Take from me my love
I will say it cannot be done

Ask my meaningless opinion
Symmetry in feelings
Positives balanced with negatives

The expanse of the mind
Is greater than that of the universe.
People's imaginations have always travelled far beyond their own two feet.
To other dimensions, worlds, places, possibilities and realities.
Only to think and be there.
What an amazing thing.

The possibilities open once you stop
Assigning random emotions
To everything

Because we are told we have to have a ‘feeling’ or
'opinion’
About everything and everyone

Stop. It is ok to not have
Preformed thoughts
About life

Go into it with an open
Mind and see what is there
Without a filter

Cuts burns and dehydration lasted the day

All while my interest in shade grew more

And once I finally achieved it
I could not stop talking about the heat

I felt like it owned a part of my soul
A part that would bend and flex[3]

---

[3] This was written after a 'foolish' trip to climb in Skaha in July... 45C of shimmering, rubber-melting heat

Only when I
Feel the room sway
And the floor beckon

To me like a ghostly
Lighthouse in the fog

And all my emotional defences
Are taken down
And hung out to dry

Will writing be an honest venture

On my hand is drawn an eye
So that I may see without lights

On my eye is tattooed a hand
So I may feel without touching

To dim a room for a darkened soul

To light up a life with a look

My lips always parting in a crooked smile, chopping out the mundane
To knead in unexpected humanity

The body of a poem
Scarred and bruised from editing
From places where it just
' Wasn't good enough '

The conclusion of a poem
A quick snap of fingers
A door slammed
A ironic sour smile in the darkness

The intro of a poem
Where nothingness lurks
The start of something big or small
Or nothing at all

Because you will find yourself at the liquor store
Using coupons you found in your neighbours mailbox

To make cheap wine cheaper
To make those deep feelings deeper

I escape my room
Slowly and with effort
I escape my room

To go somewhere
To get cheap coffee
Late at night

The lights are only candles
Littering the tables like tiny stars
To dark to read

I watch people interwoven
Leaning closer to talk
Over their table's tiny star

The night folds around me
The cold an invitation
To make yourself cosy

The cost to escape my room
$4.25
It was worthwhile for the moment[4]

---

[4] I wrote this in a late night coffee shop across from the UofA campus in 2014, little did I know how much that neighbourhood would saturate my life in the next year.

Fuel dripping from the exhaust
A shoreline radically expanding
To the left and the right

The old jalopy, worn and familiar,
Is older than the inhabitants
IT has seen its share of shorelines

But those inhabitants
Those young lovers, all alone
Are struck by the vastness of the space

They have never seen the sea
Never walked the fading grass and sand.
Drank the salt from the air with each breath, hungry for more.

They are new, untethered, free
Wild to roam where they will
In their worn jalopy.

Together they forget the world
And see the land the sea the sky
Without anywhere to be.

A low noise, like the noise of a dying man
Taking his last breath
Comes from the tires.

The car settles
The sky clouds
Rain washes away the memories.

The salt still soaks the air

Now for the ones going overboard
The water will be cold
Colder than anything you have experienced

The unfortunate truth is
You may never recover
This day may haunt you forever

But you still have to jump
Go over into the abyss
Leave this burning wreckage

And don't go back
Because the ship will not be made
Better by you leaving it

Truly the spectre of love
Must rise out of the graveyard of past wrongs and heartbreak

And bestow upon us once again
A familiar infection that will never fully leave

Even if more gravestones are promised to rise
As they always do

Fuel my ego
Watch the flames build
Too much
Will burn down the bed
Too little
Will turn it to ice instead
Fuel my ego
Watch me burn

I get permanent dimple lines and crows feet
From smiling all of the time

But the circles under my eyes
Speak plainly of painful memories

The only way to numb the past
Is to find joy in everything

People judge me for being too positive
But they don't know that

While I laugh the loudest
I also cry the hardest

There was a man
Who ate only the petals
Of the world's most beautiful flower

Every day he plucked petals for himself
And shed a tear
For each petal

When asked why he cried
He said;

"Because I disfigure the beautiful in order to live"

Often we wait
For a single
Defining moment

Where the universe
Opens up
And we gain some new revelation

About ourselves
Or others
Or something unknown

The unfortunate truth is
That this will probably
never happen

Your revelation will
Come slowly
Over time
With great pain

Because through pain
We learn new things
About ourselves

I am a skeleton of flowers
Dancing in the breeze
Flowing through time
With a cloud of bees

The bees are people
That feed off of my
Happiness
Kindness
Selflessness

But they forget that I am just a skeleton of flowers
Dancing in the breeze
One day they will eat all of me
And I will cease to be

Why have I been shelved, put away
I can't write
I can only breathe my words
Into the air and hope you listen
To the dust coming from the shelf
Wanting to be shuffled through
To feel your mind reading what you have been looking for
But the lines in my life
The dark topography is too much
I would be a forest you would not emerge from
Without scratches from my branches
And dirt on your bare feet
I am selfish with my foliage and would have you explore anyway
But to hurt you more would mean my destruction
So I stay confused
And shelved
And not explored
And you stay safe

Wander
Think
Wander
Think

Blue moon hidden by city lights
Hard stone wall hidden by a sea of concrete
Precious time passing with each breath out
Chimes in the wind
Shear through my soul with every ring to the night

Bright boxes with light
Boxes with wheels
Boxes race by in the night

Feeling numb from these past months

What are strangers?

People
We
May
Never
See
Again

So I want them to remember my smile for the rest of the day

I gave my whole heart and my soul
Poured it into a mold
Gave it life with fire
Put it high up for everyone to see
To see this thing that I lived for
And to watch it slowly crumble
I watched the pieces fall into a ocean of indifference
Saw the lack of caring in your eyes
Saw the overflowing emotions clog our view
I dove to the bottom
Gathered my soul and my heart
And kept them for myself

My little brother is in town
I took him to a record store
He bought a 'Deep Purple - Greatest Hits' album
And I walked away with 'Father John Misty'

He told me about the I.V. in his arm
How it hurts and how it'll be out soon
I got him coffee at my favourite shop
We walked around for awhile longer
He went back to the hospital
I went to work

Hopefully he will enjoy his album

Things seem so monumental before they are looked at from another perspective

Change your eyes before you back down from something that is meant for you

Change your ears before you hear only what you want to

Change your nose before it gets used to the smell of toxic relationships

Change your fingertips before they become so calloused that they hurt the ones you love

Change your lips before they lose their colour kissing someone who doesn't deserve it

Change your mind before something glues it in place forever

Change your tired feet before they sink into the mud of complacency and never recover their spring and jump

What is changed may never be
What you truly wanted to be different

But the needed constants
Are weeded out
Undesirable

Change may define you
Shake your soul
Shape it

I want to feel you
Like you can feel the indents
Of pencil lines
Flooding the writers page

Streaks and curves
Laying tangled in a
Matrix of ink and graphite

I want to paint you
Cover your body in colour
Soothe the mental scars
With drips from watercolour brushes

Every line
A watercolour droplet
Traveling your sun-kissed skin

I want to take your picture
But the light in your eyes
Would burn away the camera

Firecrackers springing
From your fingertips
Nails short from adventures

I feel love for the open spaces
For places that actually
Get dark at night

Places with bugs and larger living things
Other than humans

I love the way trees sound
When they sway with the wind
All in unison

Give me sunsets between peaks
And streets sparsely populated

Give me my home
Give me a way to endure the city

The man sits with a small brush
Dips it
And perfects the transition

Whitewashed walls
Fit for mirrors and frames and pictures
Adorned with dark red before
Now washed clean

You can see where the hired brush faltered
Where the roller lost paint
Nicks and crevasses in the wall
Still have red paint from before

They look out of place
Out of memory
Something undesirable

So the man sits with his small brush
And dips it once again
To perfect the transition

I want to wear hoodies and drink smoothies
With dirty hands
Eat Saskatoon berries from the side of the road
Drink from mountain streams
Slide and roll down mossy banks of creeks and go skinny dipping in glacier water
Have fires on the beach to dry out my wet clothes
Spend whole days climbing in the baking hot sun
Hitchhike from town to town
Get sunburned and use Aloe Vera to soothe it

While days of neglect
And lives torn apart
By misplaced love
Children's broken hearts

Lovely lights
Shining in the dark
Cold air
Warming with the offset axis
Turning our hemisphere
Toward the sun

That won't wake the children
With the broken hearts
On this day of neglect

Listen to the seasons turn
Because love will come back to you
Listen to the days of neglect
Turn to days of fulfillment and joy

I'm spreading yellow paint on toast and pretending it's mustard.

Leave me toothpaste and I will glue up temporary flowers to your bathroom walls.

Keep me sedated and I will drool obscenities into your carpet.

I'm letting all the bugs in the screen door because I ripped it.

I'm keeping all the keys to my car locked away inside it.

Insanity comes with a fever and I've had one for two weeks.

Give me love and comfort, for all that is green in my world is gone.

I'm sick, pardon me…

A rush of bright light
Pulses though
My soul

Matching my heartbeat
Goosebumps
I can feel them in my jaw

Violins
Pull my soul up
By the scruff of my neck
Out of depression

Too much
Tears
Flow from my ears

Perfect as my night sky
Lights up with light
Pulsing with my heartbeat

Water runs
Saline and imperfect
Down a sun drenched face
Covered in dirt
White teeth
Cracked lips like the edge of a now dormant volcano

Keep your eyes up
Keep them fixed on that horizon
Broken and fissured
By a mountain skyline

Live my love
Like the wanderers of old
Keep your eyes ready
To see life lift it's hazy morning fog
To reveal a bright new day

I feel anger at people and things that I used to love.
I feel disconnection from most people.
I feel lost in my pursuit of goals.
I feel a need to re-connect with my feelings of life and simple nature that I used to love.

Pouring myself into a unsustainable job hurt my values and re-arranged my morals.
Now that I no longer have that job, I'm finding it very difficult to reconcile my career goals with the amount of reckless consumerism rampant in my chosen career.
I want to do something different with my skill set, but I feel a little bit scared of what I might have to do to 'live without regret'.
I must re-align my interests with my career and my souls desires.

For some time the planets have been turning and turning
Let's start spinning the wheels on this station wagon
This idea machine
This escape from a boring destiny
This affront to all things clean and soft and 'high-brow'

Let's set up camp with people we have never met
Let's sleep by the fire
By the water
In the cold air awaken to kiss with frosted lips
And watch the planets track their old paths across the sky
And let us vow never to sink into routine.

"You know the way into my heart."

"I know." Her voice cracked with a smile

"I've traveled that road many times"

Stacks and stacks
Years folded in frozen tales of scattered light reflecting off of a sea of timeless ice

Feeling distant from the world
Apart from its tales
A lonely soulful glacier
Sends envoys of icebergs
Slowly toward the sea

Stacks and stacks
Time forever frozen in its heart
Layered and folded
The forerunner of the glacier
Our lonely iceberg
Sails out to sea

Only as the warmer oceans embrace
Slowly washes him away
Does he understand that he will never make it back to the glacier

Unshakeable from its task
The iceberg travels onward
A forgotten envoy
To a world that has no more love of ice or snow[5]

---

[5] I wrote this poem on the black sand beaches of Jökulsárlón, 2015, while among the icebergs

I like what my hands say 'Simply let me be'
Let me live
I just want to be Me

A chorus reverberates through existence
It comes from the Stars
You can hear them sing on clear nights
When the clouds do not muffle their voices

If you listen you can hear their harmony
Older than the earth
Older than the sea
Far older than you or me

If they notice you listening
They will sing to you
They will make a song of your life
Show you what you can do
With the little time you have

Listen to our Stars
They wont lead you astray
They will comfort your weary soul
They will sing you to sleep

Listen to the trees
They sing to each other
They use the wind
To carry their voices from their leaves

Whispers in the trees
Whispers in the leaves
The winter wind is coming
When the trees will start their longings
For spring to come again

But now in Autumn
The trees celebrate the summer
Celebrate the sun and rain
They know it will come again

But until then
They will talk while they still have voices
Whispers of good green things
Listen to the trees

Desire is what I keep
Hidden like a solar flare
I burn brightly
Watch Me Care

The smell of shirts days old
Something of a memory passes over your mind
You remember when you mind, body and soul were one
Only and ever one, you slept on the road without worry

Keep your worries alive
Or so they say
Because if you forget them
They won't be able to keep you
From being free

Caught unawares by night
Our minds invent ways
through which we may
Experience what we could not
During the day

That game can keep you camped out on the line
Between life and insanity
Keep your body whole
Don't stop playing
Don't stop to think

Just roll

Sometimes the words
Just come out wrong

Sometimes life
Just goes along and along and along

Pouring over and over
Limitless they oscillate
One with the wild nature of their desires
Plans constantly changing

They gather and separate
Trying on others like old coats
Best when still warm from those previous
They talk grim and grimy of the 'competition'

Our Society
This gross approximation of 'Order'
Separation created by a flawed perception

But while they are condemned by themselves
The sport is participated by the majority
Lives torn and put back together
By this frame of distance and certainty in the future
Without a thought to the 'unknown'

But sailing, they do not look towards the shore
But rather thrust their heads under the waves
Believing that there is no land for this ship
Diving into the water
Down
Down
Down
Until they forget the land
The sun
The life giving air
As they swim...
Pouring in and out of the water
Limitless they oscillate

One with the wild nature of the waves

You could save your wings
You could tie them together out of sight
Out of mind
You could preserve them
Keep them safe

Or you could let them stretch and stretch
Until they reach out and block the morning sun
And you could fly

And as you flew you would lose some feathers
It would hurt a lot
But they would always grow back stronger
And you would be better off

You would soar and feel freedom
If in exchange for some pain

The light from the setting sun
Would not throw shadows that could touch you
So high up you would be.

Never let my mind become
Old and grey
Like photos of summers long gone

Never let my mind become tired of feeling
For we do not pick emotions
"I want this one, I want that one"

Let my mind become
Like a beacon in a avalanche rescue
Always needed
Always on

I saw a thousand frozen lakes today
Breaking in the sun

I saw a million trees today
Thawing one by one

I glimpsed the sun
Unhindered by clouds
Warming everyone

If I had wings I would fly towards a sunset that I
cannot see
I would search the oceans for a place where my mind
cannot follow me

In the morning I would wake as if next to a lover
And the world would open for me and show me
instead

White shores with black sand
And I would meet myself there

The part of me that I haven't seen in a long time

And we would go swimming

I am a leaf in the wind
Time doesn't bother me
Because I am free

I am a leaf in the wind
Watch me be me

I am a leaf in the wind
Love is my reality
It will never cease to be

We are just snowflakes
Drifting in a season of endless change

Helpless to the whims of reality
Flying in a sky of endless possibility

These moments can seem like years
Dragging on with a lethargic pace

Or if you choose, these moments
Can seem like a brief interlude to an even greater possibly

You can decide for yourself
But I will spend them with love in my heart
Open to the possibilities before me

Because when Winter and Summer
Spill themselves across your window panes

I hope again and again
That the love I gave
Would be felt

In the softness of the snow
And in the warmth of the morning sun

When truth steps down
From my open window pane
The cold air
Blossoming across
My bed frame
The silence is absolute
But my soul knows the language
Keeping in time with the rhythm
I move and flow
My dreams
They answer my waking questions
With absolute uncertainty
I wake up
Feeling better
Feeling nothing
But silence
And cold air

Your smile reflects the same light that comes from inside your soul

A small pinprick
Letting out a little light
A glimpse
At the star
Beneath your surface

Your smile is fire in my stomach
And ice on my neck

Peaceful and calming
Light in a deep night

I want to drink deep
From a well of self realization
That I am the beginning
And the end
Of my story

I bled forced tears upon a silver plate
Exiled plans forced to wait in purgatory
Through no fault of their own
Watching watches watch the sun slip down
Time
Is a gift
To be squandered with unrivalled selfishness
Wasted inside a maze mind
Trying to find my soul
Feeling the unravelled strands of emotion
And tying it up with hope
This century
Keeps on delivering the most surprises

I watched but did not speak it
Scared of the past repeated
And so it came with a bang
A sudden slap of reality
I wilted

But now my path runs forward
Now plans made
Are coming to fruition
I grow
I am

Leaving expectation behind
I dive towards the unknown
Fearlessly keeping time
Building up my soul

The sunset happens many times
In the desert
I watched the light flow down the volcanic rock

As it burned my nose for one last second
I wished I could have had one second more

To deny the darkness my headlamp
And to sit and watch the stars poke through the oxygen
barrier

Talking in the back yard
Like we're not pretty small
Like we've got it all
As if our one tiny experience
Is all that there is

Something more exists
Out beyond the mists
Simply unreachable
Because we have decided it is so

Alone or together
Time passes at the same rate
Leaving us with what we decided to learn
Explore and experience

I think I'll stop pushing
Away things that could happen today
And let my small experience
Open up myself more than yesterday

Still smooth the message spreads
Like rubbing charcoal across your back
Grains ripping into your skin
Blood turning black

What is love but a way to share your life
A meaning saturated into every day activities
A sorrow at the sudden loss of connection
A bleeding at every unwanted turn
A sad longing for what was before
And will be again

What is love but the look of utter belonging
Pouring out from their eyes
Like a facet barely able to keep up with the volume of the pour

Keeping an openness is hard
So very very hard
When your instincts tell you to turn away
Turn off

But what is love
But that commitment to keep your heart open
No matter what happens
To commit to not giving up
Even when they give up on you

That is love in my eyes
That is what my mind always thinks about
It is always a wonder

Irresistible
Isn't it?

Keeping tabs on my memories
Those happy ones
The sad ones too
Over and Over

Keeping tabs on my memories
How come we play with time
Some things are too soon
Some things are too late

My face is stuffed with memories
They choke me to death
While I hold them in

I got up to wander
My mind in a daze
The haze extending to my body
I'm sick
And my dreams are not safe anymore

That's what is difficult
Stars and sheets
Bird calls and beautiful trees
The snow from a cloudy sky

Like a tenth as precious
Without you there to watch the snow
Coalesce into a single new form
Quietly coating the forest floor

As if my experience in life is lessened
Greatly by your absence

I yearn for your affection
Validation of the worth of my experience
Was found in your eyes

A mental bock

Stopping me
Myself
This expectation is
Blocking me

I expect this to be the same
As the last time
As the last 40 tries
Before

People crushing
Before me
It is hard to not compare
Myself and despair

But I do what I can
Bleeding over the week
Into the world with fingers bruised
Blackened resolve

Running with my fears
Throughout my experiences
That no one can see

I feel like an idiot
Weaving words
Beneath slivered glass
A copy
Shit
This emblem of accomplishment
Covering
Saving futures that will never happen
Creating a nothingness
That never ceases to be

I feel a profound need to be loved
By myself
By others
Never enough
It's never enough
I'm always exposed
Fear creeping
Through my shield
Wide eyes
Screaming into the dark

I love to include people
To bring them together
To watch from afar
Once I have finished what I have accomplished
And then leave once it's done

I find it hard to fully include myself
The time and stress and effort
Seems wasted on myself

But I am learning to love my own company
To leave behind things
Values and attitudes
That hinder my soul from growing

So don't ask me why I am always walled off
When I was the one who planned the trip
I have to still figure out
If opening up
Is a valuable thing to do

There are words
Written in the silence
Between your last breath
And the next

Words only you can hear
If you are quiet enough
To understand
The mind of a water droplet
Evaporating from the ocean

Particle values
Lost through translation
Of dissonant sounds
Into meaningful melodies

Cherish these values
Lost to order
Born of inharmonious beginnings

They speak from the past
Moving towards the future
Always towards chaos

And as you wake
Joyful sunset
To your thoughtless haunts
Greatly growing movement
Towards leafy greens
The promise like a threat
Hanging over the comfort and relaxation
That strangles to death
I will move
Keeping on

Two faces
Split
Apposing lines
Fractions of time
Composing my soul
As far as I can go
Around and around
My head
Far and away
My heart soars
Wait..
There might be more

How many people have
Held sunlight in their souls
Just to have it
When the night comes
So they will be able to see
Through the dark

You tell yourself
It won't happen
Haha never
And then it happens
And the world emboweled
Bleeds across the bluest of skies
Staining an ever growing list of
Cant's

Like an itch
The urge to leave
Depart completely and with haste
As if from a bank heist
Jewels of time meant to be wasted
Slipping from overfilled fingers
Clutching grasping
Whispering "leave "

Far and above
As a fish under the water
Watching those above the surface
Achieve fulfillment and dreams
Whilst I, waterlogged and wasteful
Plumb the depths of my uncaring soul
For pearls of passion

Flowing far flung rivers
Arrive at their destination
Only to be absorbed by the collective
And regress from their autonomy
Shattered dreams of eternal flow
Fade from the depths of deep near-delta shores

I feel like
My body contains 4 skeletons
Under one skin
And letting them all
Live together
Is harder than letting just
One win

Spilling fantasy
From between my ribs
As if from multiple puncture wounds

My little thoughts congealed
Around each and every opening
Sutures of self control
Sustain my soul

For long enough
Until it can leave me
Self hatred and a monopoly of doubt
Shred my emotional muscles
Into a meaty shaking pulp

It's that I feel

Morose, wistfully gazing towards something

Similar to before
An ache
Forms where I thought it would never
And sealed inside
Is a heartbeat
That will never stop skipping

Wistful and with longing
I turn away
Into another
Sunset
Alone

The setting sun
Blasted the rock wall
Into shadows and splinters of light
Red and vibrant
As if lightning had struck
And turned stone
Into fodder for the fire

Things that seem commonplace
Things that I do on a weekly basis
Are things that my past self would be so surprised
To see me be comfortable with

Life is simply telling me
To let the things that scare me
Take me away
To something that I can't even dream about

Thin lines
The confluence of major weakness
The shame of the smoothness
The wrinkle
The trough

All become the focal point
Become the important areas for a climber
We look for the imperfections
In the rock
To lead us forward

And that is true for more than just climbing
You are not only your strengths
But also your 'weaknesses'
And they propel you

I just can't explain
Simple things just take
All my confusion
And make it fall away
Just like rain

Largely because of my
Inability to have a bad attitude
Or terrible thoughts
In sunshine dispersed
Through the trees

Do I subconsciously try to keep
Myself from trees
And sunshine

And it never works

I've enjoyed my brain
Now take it from me
I'd like to go insane

Hehe too free
Accented
Return please
To my unfailing repression
Of my best qualities

Vapid and discontent
I wander the options
Presented to me
By those without any left
For themselves
Early in the morning
I ponder
Things I hope never to do

You Oxford rough
Made of sandals
and wild sentiment

Pillaging the future
Of things better left in the past

My composure
Slips away always
Revealing a half mad intuition
And a razor sharp wit

The memory of the pain
Like a scab ripped off too quickly
Will burn red for a time
Until it too fades like water
In hot sand

Arching feelings
The absence of pain
Encourages disconnection
Rooted within all of us
Is the ability to let go
If we are pushed far enough

Waterfall though stone lungs
The breath encompassing
Indescribable
Feeling in all directions

Do not put your past selves down
Do not drown them in contempt
For the situations and circumstances
Like water from the sky
Were not under your control

You are now evolved
But do not disassociate yourself
From who you became
In order to survive

They are like small children
Huddled inside you
Nurture them back into the open
Let them see that you have become
Someone who can protect them

Then you will know peace from the past
And life with yourself
Will brighten into the future

90049991R00079

Made in the USA
Columbia, SC
07 March 2018